For

GW01045144

Sea Fishing Knots
From the **reel** to the **hook**

ISBN/EAN : 978-90-71747-27-4

Whatever your angling passion,
whether it's light rock fishing
or chasing big fish with big lures,
you should be able to find the
right sea fishing knot here.

Clear, concise, easy to follow
illustrations that should help
you to gain a solid base of
reliable, tried and tested knots.

Tight lines and strong knots.

Copyright Notice

No part of this document may be
reproduced in any form or by
any means without permission
in writing from:

Contents

Sea fishing knots set-up   5
Spool knot   6
Double grinner knot   7
Improved Albright knot   8
Tournament leader knot   9
Seaguar knot   10
Grinner knot   11
Braid ring knot   12
Dropper loop   13
Lineman's loop   14
Figure 8 loop   15
Surgeon's loop   16
Loop-dropper loop   17
Palomar knot   18
Domhof knot   19
Snell knot-1   20
Snell knot-2   21
Easy snell knot   22
Half blood knot   23
Bristle boom rig knot   24
Bristle boom rig - snood knot   25
Power gum stop knot   26

Big game fishing knots set-up   27
Spool knot   28
Spider hitch knot   29
Triple surgeon's loop   30
Bimini twist   31

Contents

Cat's paw	33
Slim beauty	34
Bristol knot	35
Improved Bristol knot	36
Double uni knot	37
Simplified FG knot	38
Offshore swivel knot	41
Haywire twist	42
Flemish eye	43
Three turn thumb knot	44
Mono leader crimping	45
Fat mono knot	46
Snell knot	47
Assist hook knot	48

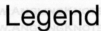

Legend

 Reel   *Pliers*

 Hook   *Super glue*

 Moisten   *Lighter*

  Trim   *Heat gun*

  Crimp   *Hold braid in mouth*

Sea Fishing Knots Set-up

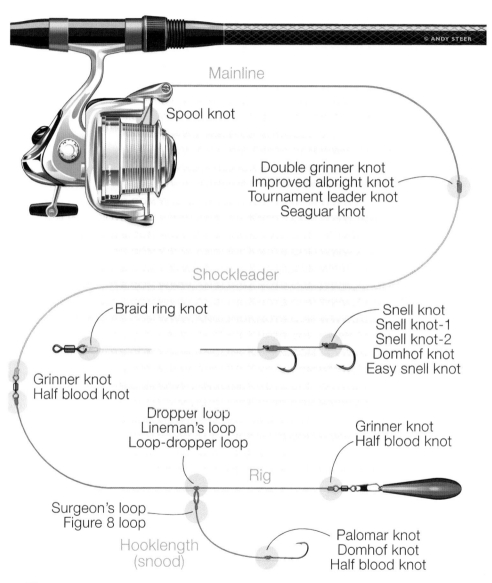

© ANDY STEER

Mainline

Spool knot

Double grinner knot
Improved albright knot
Tournament leader knot
Seaguar knot

Shockleader

Braid ring knot

Snell knot
Snell knot-1
Snell knot-2
Domhof knot
Easy snell knot

Grinner knot
Half blood knot

Dropper loop
Lineman's loop
Loop-dropper loop

Grinner knot
Half blood knot

Rig

Surgeon's loop
Figure 8 loop

Palomar knot
Domhof knot
Half blood knot

Hooklength
(snood)

The sea fishing knots set-up shows the basic sea fishing
line connections and knots.

Spool Knot

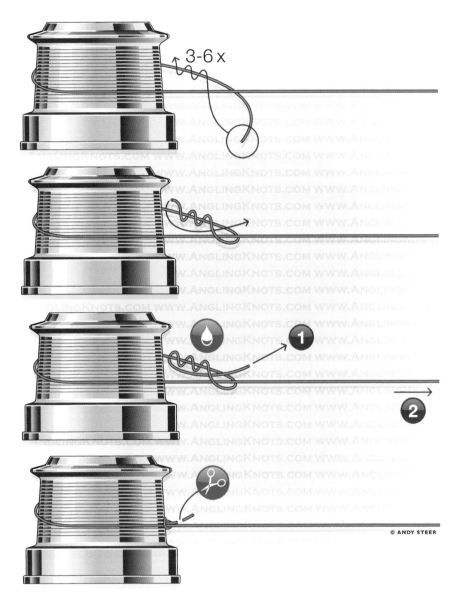

3-6 x

© ANDY STEER

The spool knot is used to attach the mainline to the spool.
When attaching braided line it's advisable to make several
extra wraps around the line.

Double Grinner Knot

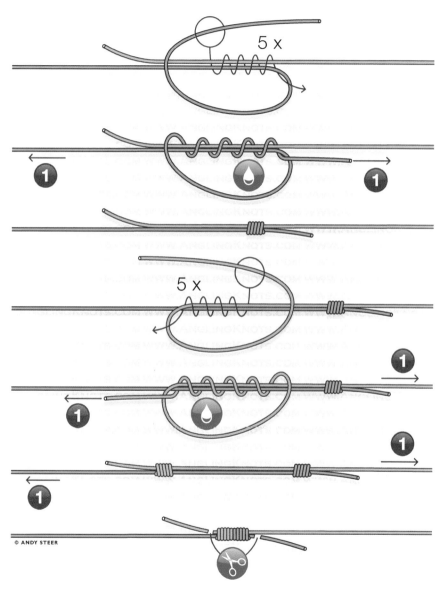

The double grinner/uni-uni knot is a good choice for joining mono to mono or mono to braid. Make five turns with mono, five to ten turns with braid.

Improved Albright Knot

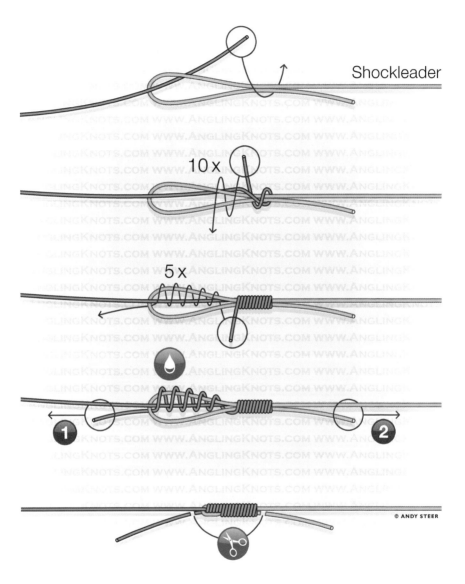

Shockleader

© ANDY STEER

The improved albright knot is a good strong connection for attaching your shock leader to the main line. A low profile knot that will readily pass through your rod rings.

Tournament Leader Knot

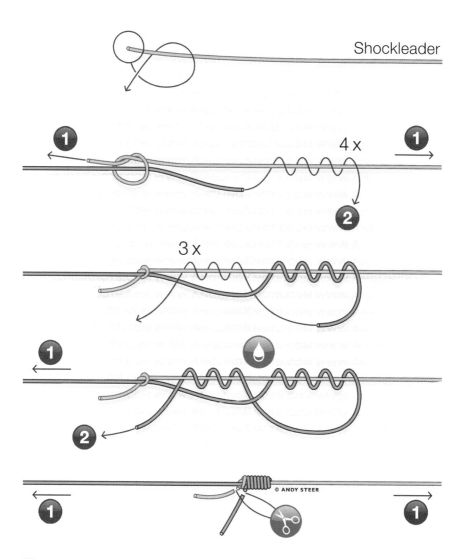

The tournament leader knot is a very strong connection for attaching your shock leader to the main line. A low profile knot that will readily pass through your rod rings.

Seaguar Knot

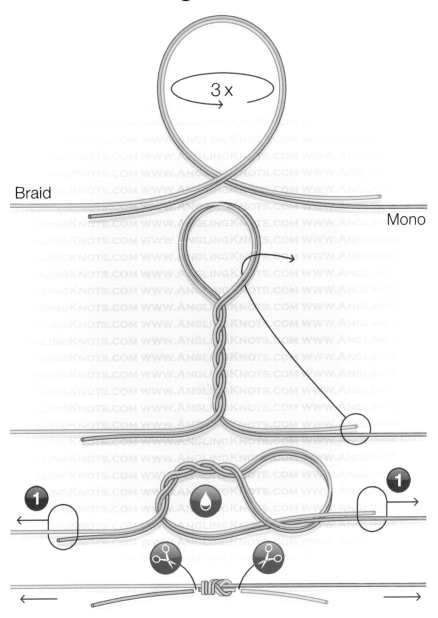

The seaguar knot, a strong, quick and easy way to connect a mono/fluorcarbon leader to braid line.

Grinner Knot

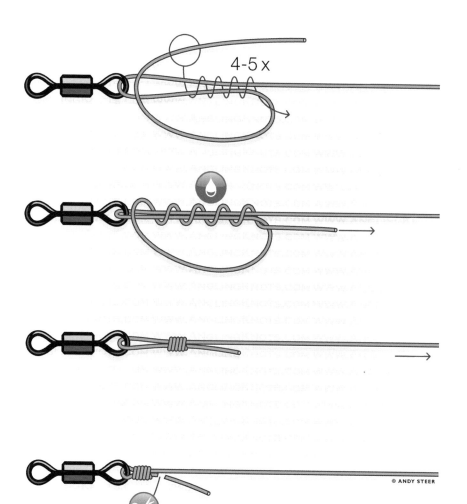

4-5 x

© ANDY STEER

The grinner knot/uni-knot is a strong and reliable knot for attaching lures, hooks and swivels.

Braid Ring Knot

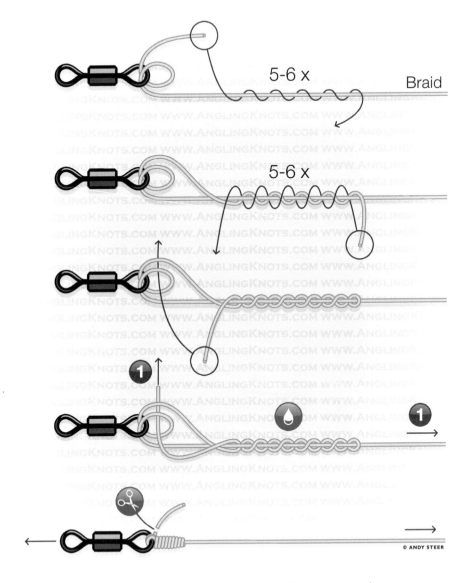

The braid ring knot is good solid knot for connecting braided line to swivels and terminal tackle.

Dropper Loop

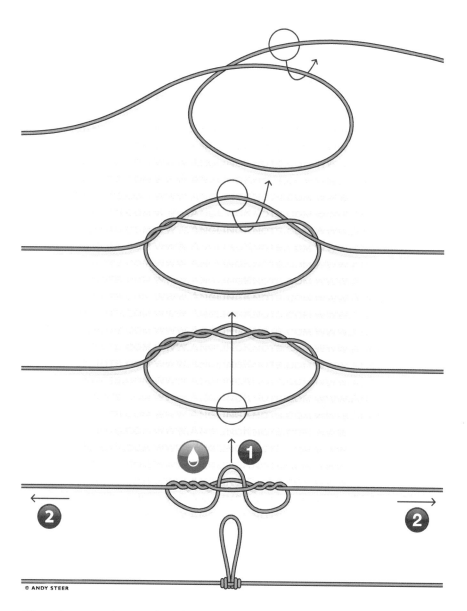

© ANDY STEER

The dropper loop aka dropper knot or blood loop knot. It's often used to make multiple hook bait rigs or to attach lures above a jig.

Lineman's Loop

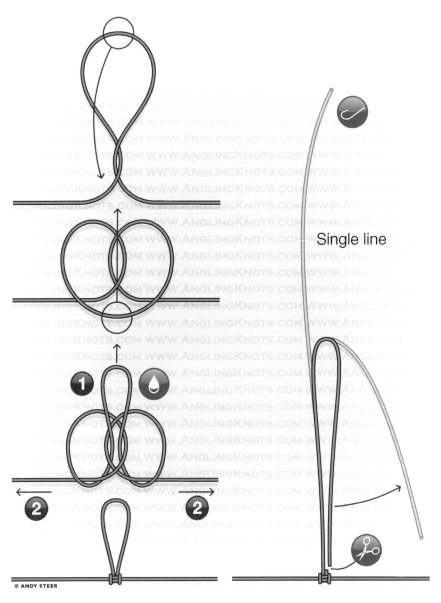

Single line

The lineman's loop. It's often used to make multiple hook bait rigs or to attach lures above a jig.

Figure 8 Loop

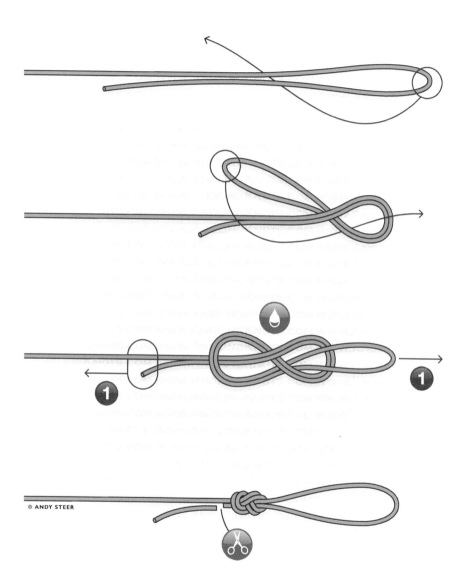

© ANDY STEER

The figure eight loop is one of the simplest ways to tie a loop. Use for loop to loop connections.

Surgeon's Loop

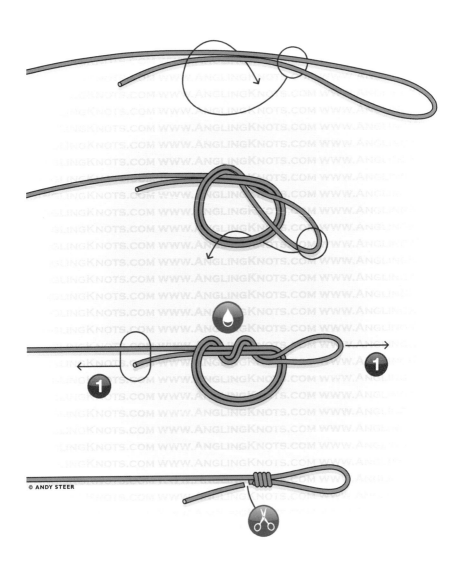

The surgeon's loop is quick and reliable way to form a loop. Use for loop to loop connections.

Loop-Dropper Loop

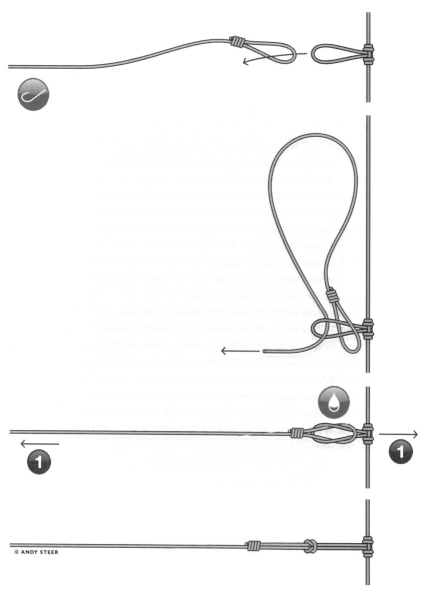

© ANDY STEER

With the loop-dropper loop connection you can easily join or change hooks and lures on the rig.

Palomar Knot

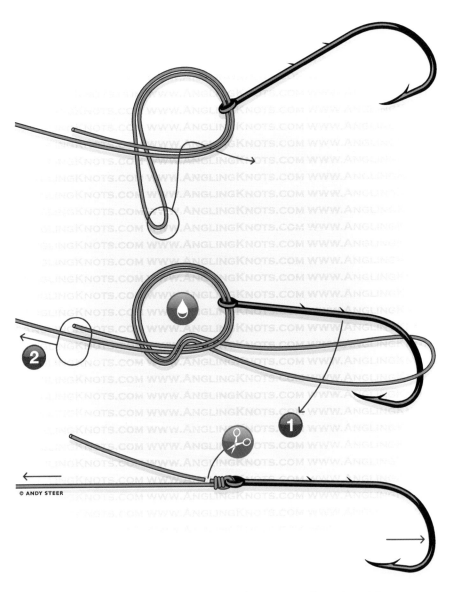

The palomar knot is a reliable and easy to tie a knot for attaching hooks and swivels.

Domhof Knot

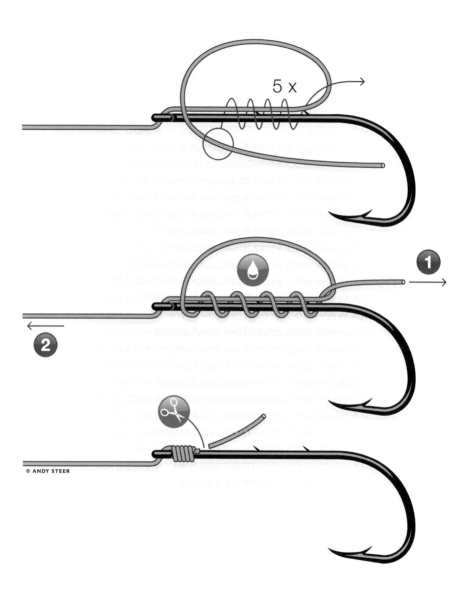

5 x

1

2

© ANDY STEER

The domhof knot is a strong and neat knot for attaching the hook.

Snell Knot-1

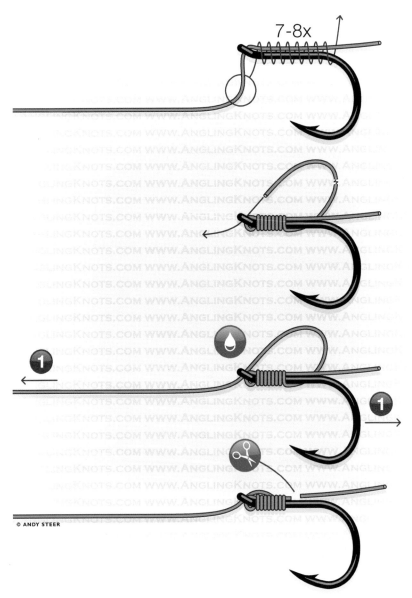

The snell knot is a exceptionally strong and reliable knot for attaching hooks.

Snell Knot-2

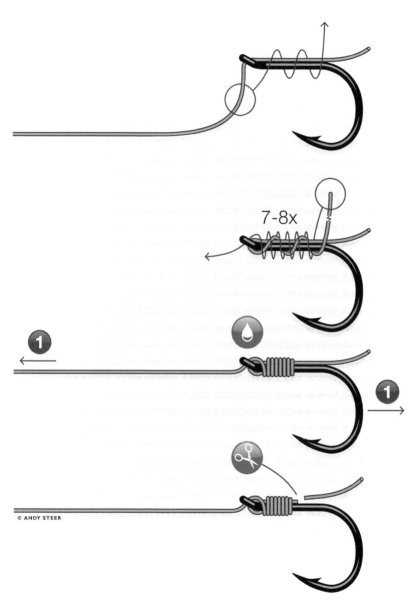

7-8x

The snell knot is a exceptionally strong and reliable knot for attaching hooks.

Easy Snell Knot

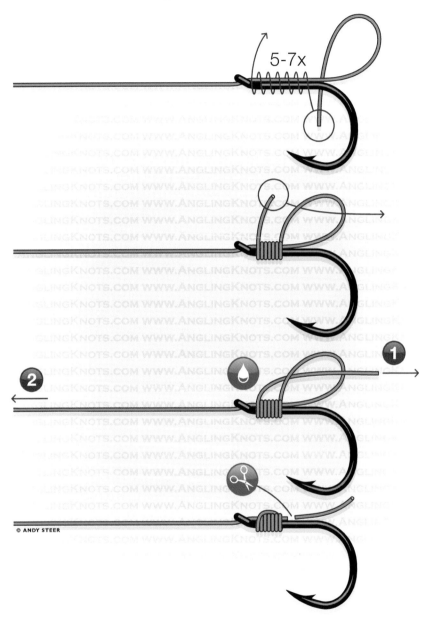

The easy snell knot, a quick and easy method for snelling a hook.

Half Blood Knot

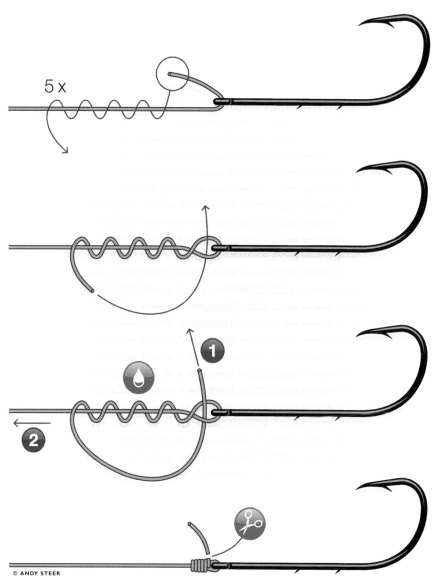

5 x

1

2

© ANDY STEER

The half turn blood knot is one of the most widely used
fishing knots for attaching the line to hooks and swivels.

Bristle Boom Rig Knot

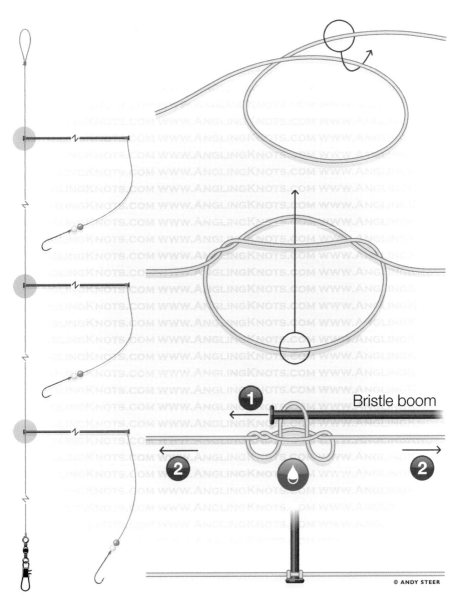

Bristle boom

Use this knot to attach the rig line to the bristle boom.

Bristle Boom Rig - Snood Knot

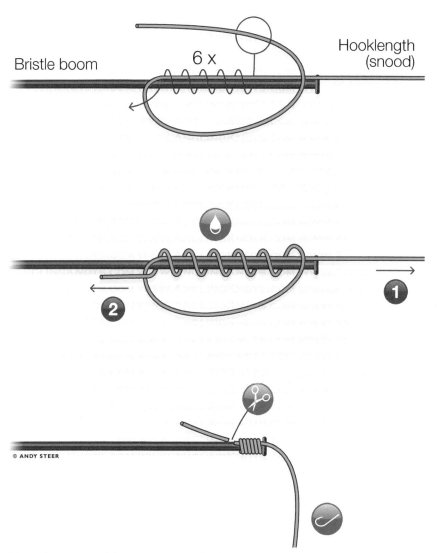

Use the snood knot to attach the hooklength to the bristle boom.

Power Gum Stop Knot

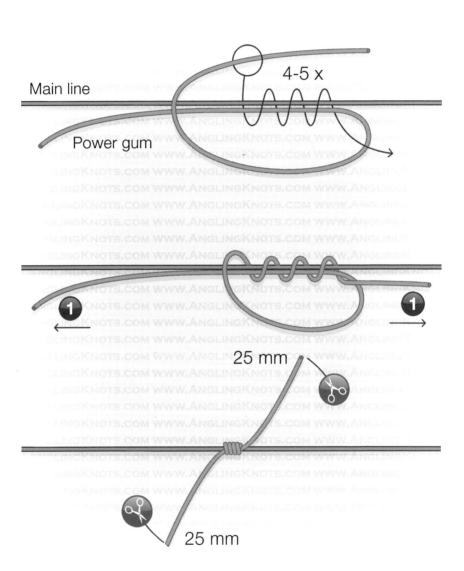

Main line

Power gum

4-5 x

1

1

25 mm

25 mm

The stop knot is the ideal knot for preventing your float from slipping. Trim the ends of the power gum to 25 mm (1 inch) so that the stop knot passes easily through the rod rings.

Big Game Fishing Knots Set-up

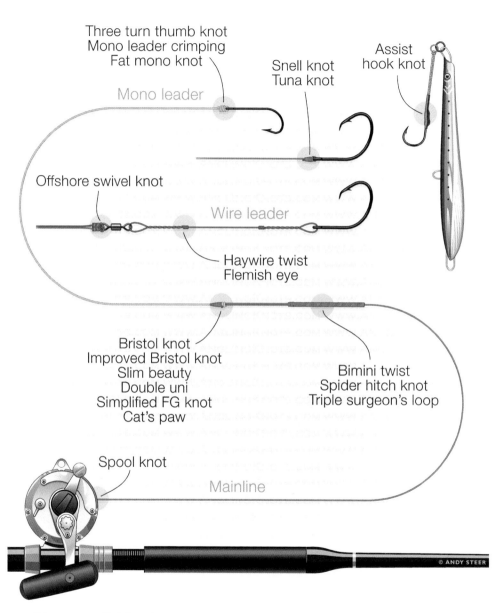

Three turn thumb knot
Mono leader crimping
Fat mono knot

Snell knot
Tuna knot

Assist
hook knot

Mono leader

Offshore swivel knot

Wire leader

Haywire twist
Flemish eye

Bristol knot
Improved Bristol knot
Slim beauty
Double uni
Simplified FG knot
Cat's paw

Bimini twist
Spider hitch knot
Triple surgeon's loop

Spool knot

Mainline

© ANDY STEER

Big game fishing knots set-up shows the basic line
connections and knots.

Spool Knot

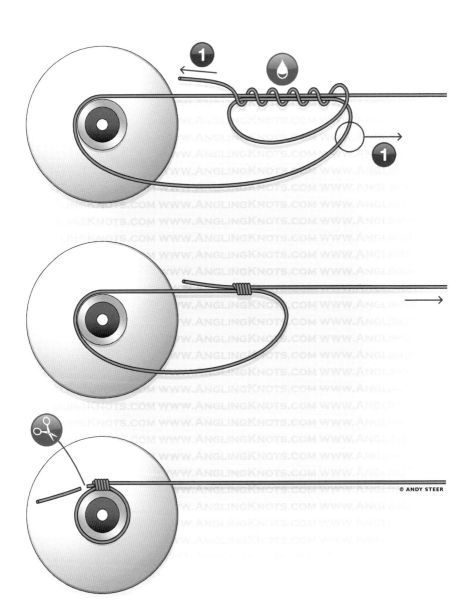

© ANDY STEER

The spool knot is used to attach the mainline to the spool.
When attaching braided line it's advisable to make
several extra wraps around the spool.

Spider Hitch Knot

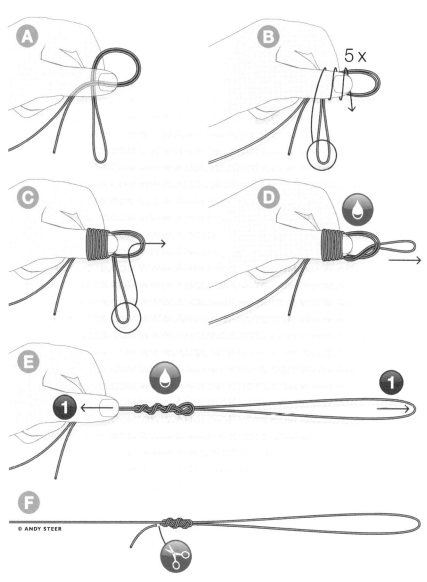

The spider hitch is an excellent knot for quickly forming a strong loop.

Triple Surgeon's Loop

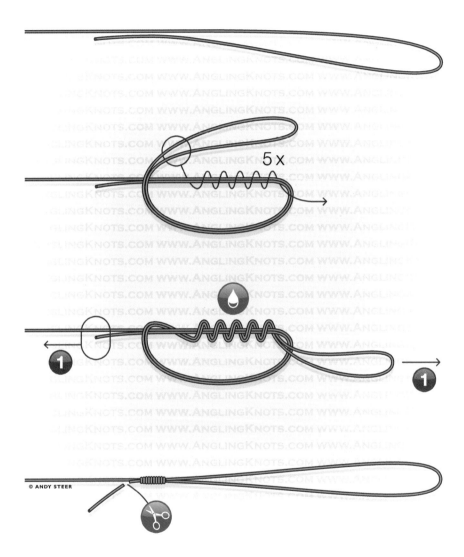

© ANDY STEER

The triple surgeon's loop is a quick and easy loop to tie.

Bimini Twist

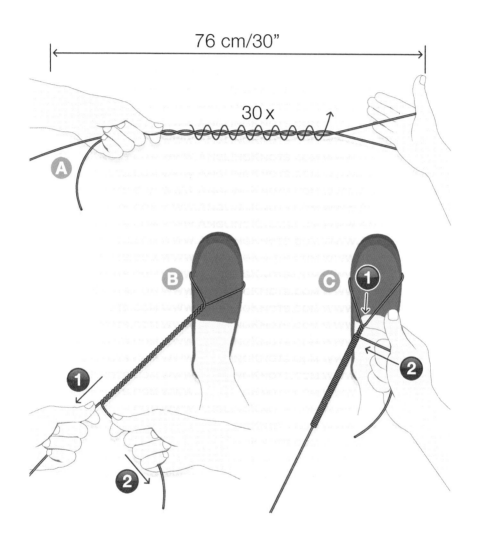

The bimini twist is considered to be the 100% strong loop.

Bimini Twist

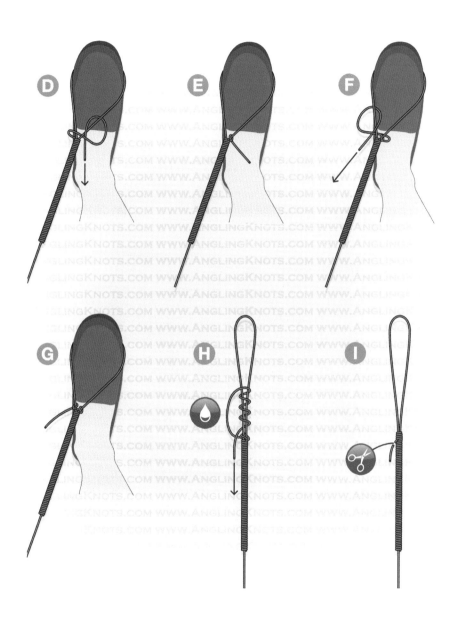

Cat's Paw

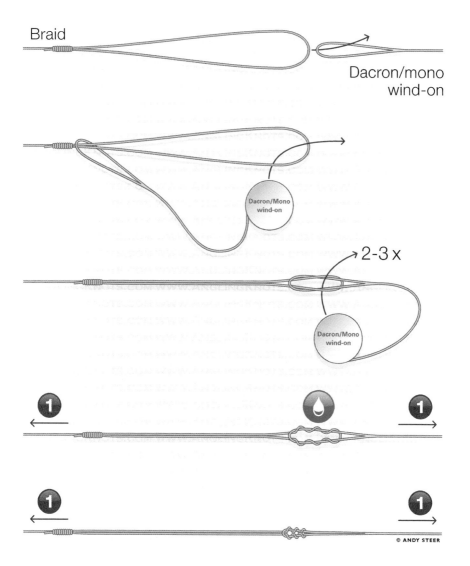

The traditional cats paw, use it to attach a double line to dacron or mono wind-ons.

Slim Beauty

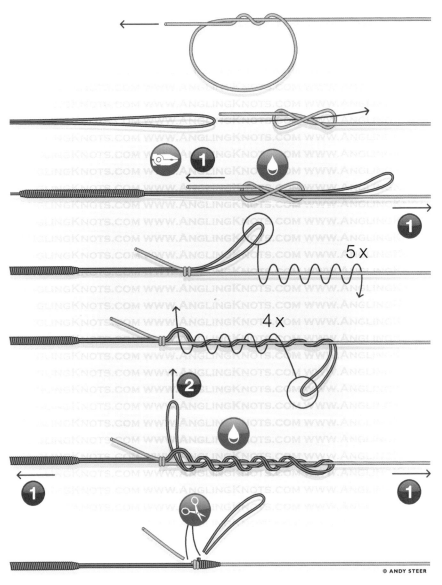

© ANDY STEER

The slim beauty knot is a strong, easy to tie low profile knot that creates a streamlined connection between a double line and leader that will smoothly pass through your rod rings.

Bristol Knot

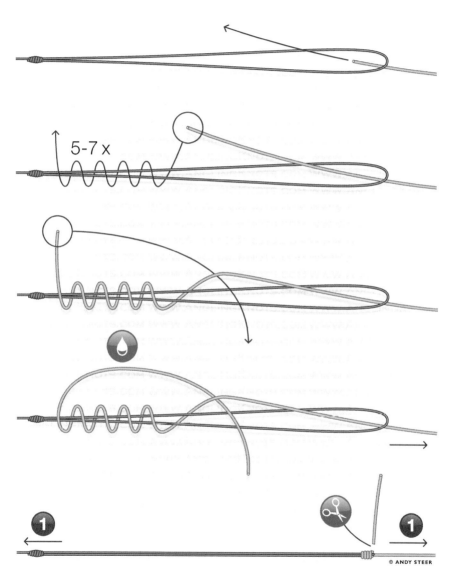

5-7 x

1

1

The Bristol knot creates a streamlined connection between a double line and leader that will smoothly pass through your rod rings.

Improved Bristol Knot

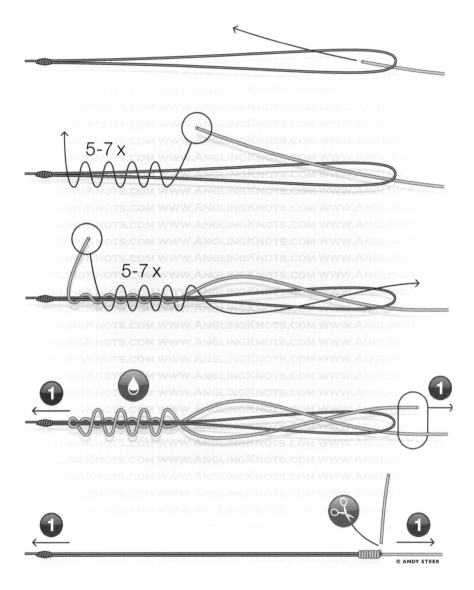

The improved Bristol knot creates a streamlined connection between a double line and leader that will smoothly pass through your rod rings.

Double Uni Knot

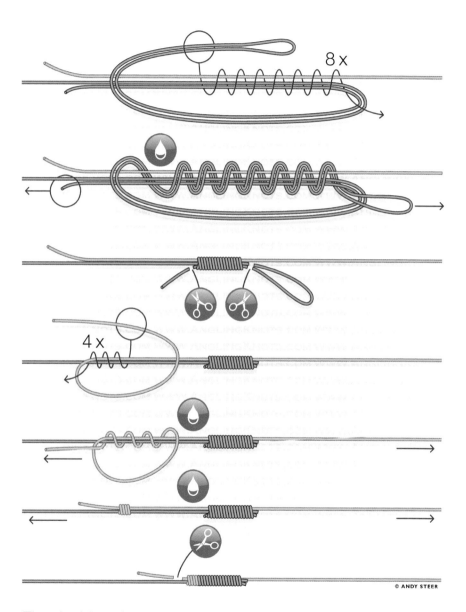

The double uni knot is a good strong knot for joining braid to a mono leader.

Simplified FG Knot

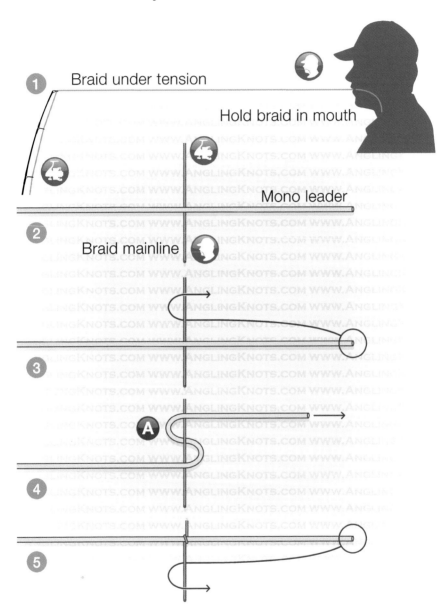

Braid under tension

Hold braid in mouth

Mono leader

Braid mainline

The simplified FG knot, a compact, very strong and dependable braid to leader knot.

Disclaimer: *No responsibility in any way is accepted for incidents arising from the use of this material.*

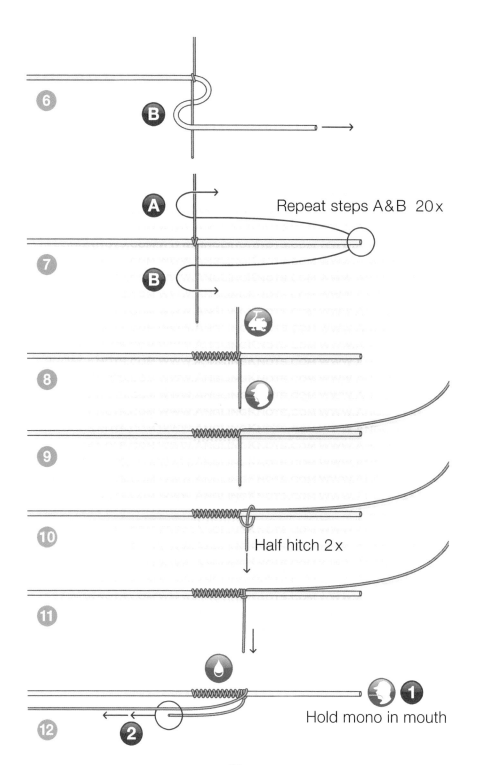

6

B

A Repeat steps A&B 20x

7

B

8

9

10 Half hitch 2x

11

12 **1** Hold mono in mouth

2

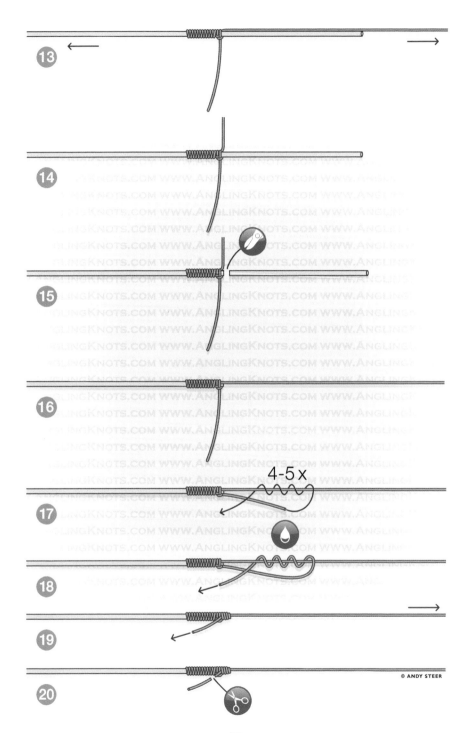

4-5 x

© ANDY STEER

40

Offshore Swivel Knot

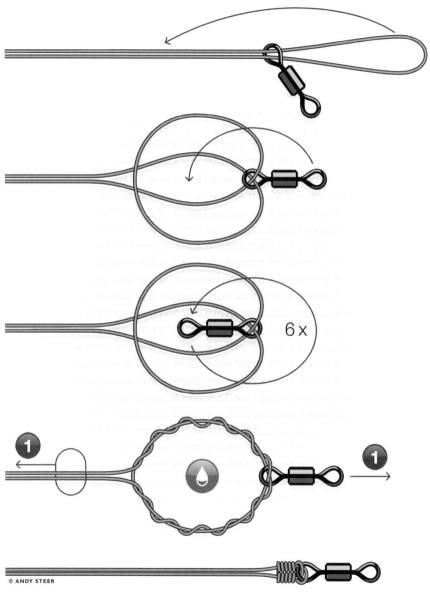

© ANDY STEER

The offshore swivel knot is used to connect a swivel to a double line. 3 loops for > 50 lb line, 4 loops for 30 lb - 50 lb line, 5 loops for 12 lb - 30 lb line, 6 loops for < 12 lb line.

Haywire Twist

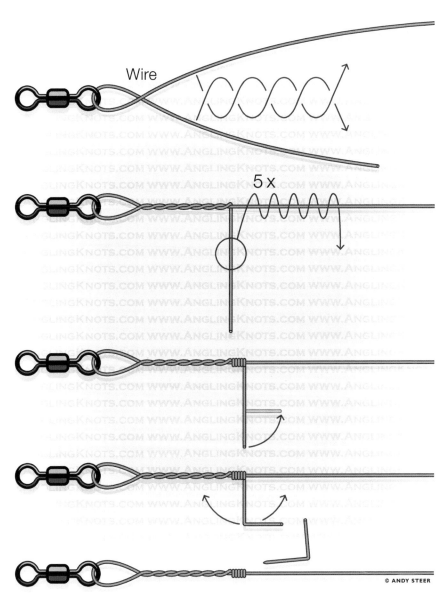

The haywire twist is the strongest connection for joining single-strand wire to a swivel, hook or lure.

Flemish Eye

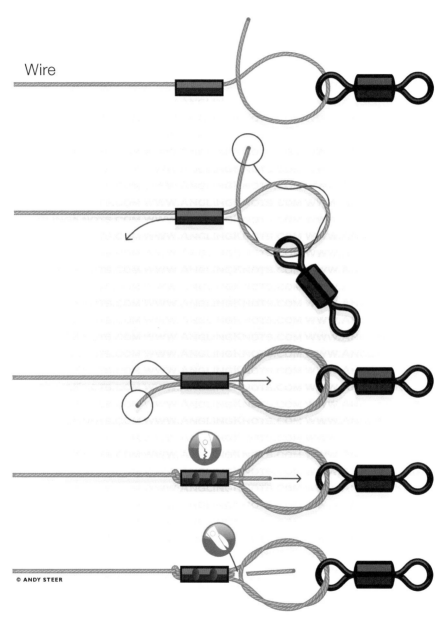

Wire

© ANDY STEER

The flemish eye aka offshore loop is used to create a
reinforced loop in a leader. It works well with stainless steel
wire or mono.

43

Three Turn Thumb Knot

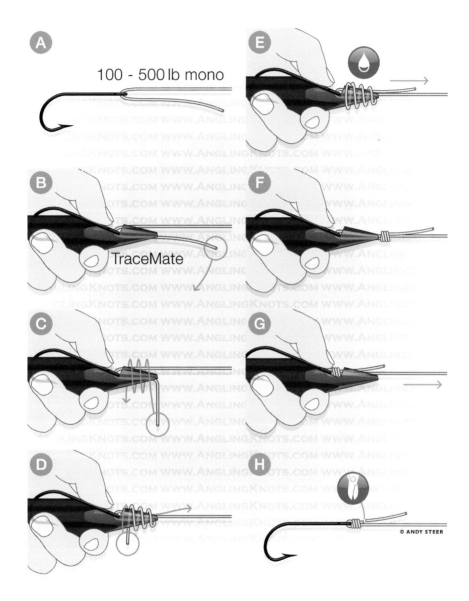

A 100 - 500 lb mono

B TraceMate

C

D

E

F

G

H

© ANDY STEER

The three turn thumb knot is probably the best knot for tying heavy mono to hooks or swivels.

Mono Leader Crimping

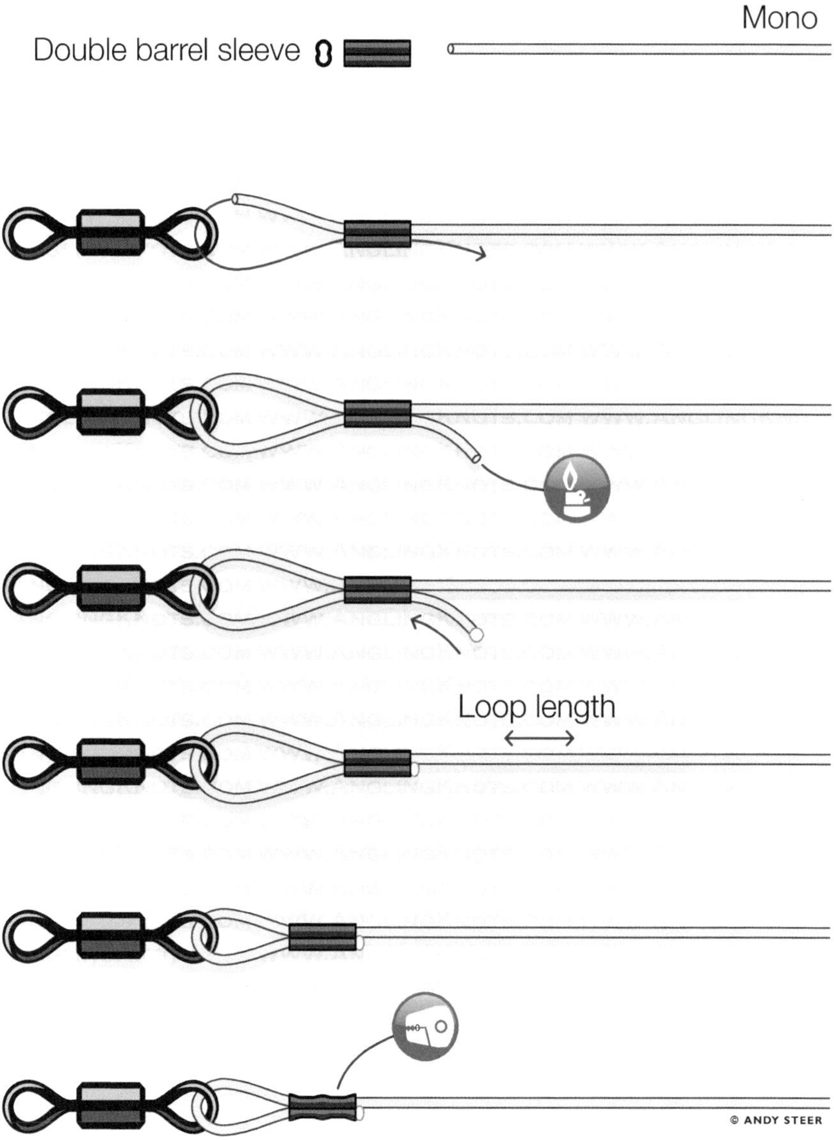

Mono
Double barrel sleeve
Loop length
© ANDY STEER

Use the mono leader crimping to create a small strong connection to swivels, clips and hooks.

Fat Mono Knot

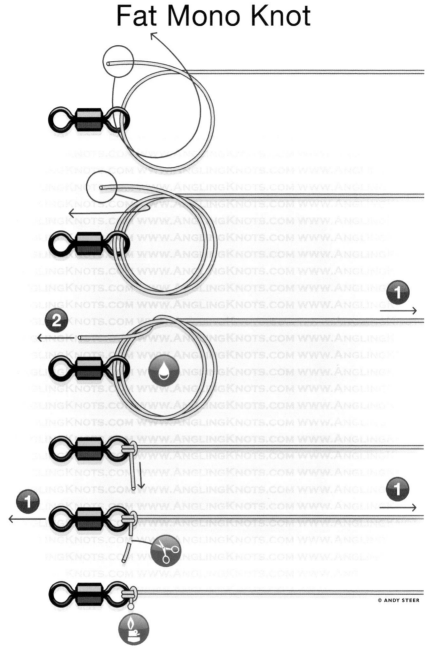

Use the Fat mono knot for attaching hooks and swivels to thick mono, hard mono en fluorcarbon line (>1,2 mm).

Snell Knot

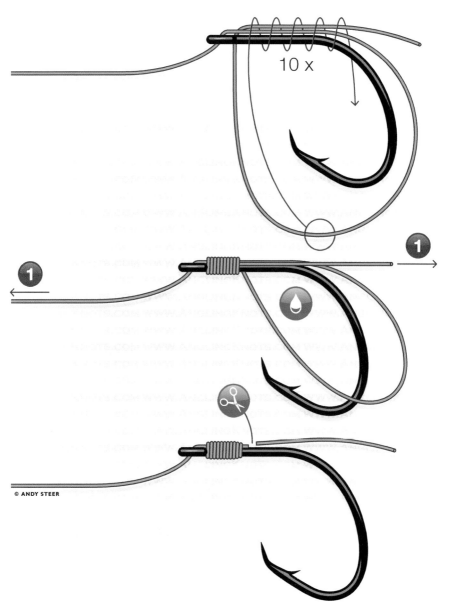

10 x

The snell knot is an exceptionally strong and reliable knot for attaching hooks.

Assist Hook Knot

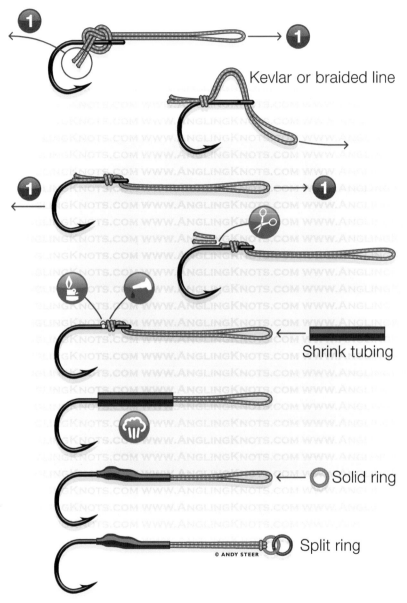

Kevlar or braided line

Shrink tubing

Solid ring

Split ring

© ANDY STEER

This is one quick and easy method to produce a reliable assist hook.

16444772R00030

Printed in Poland
by Amazon Fulfillment
Poland Sp. z o.o., Wrocław